BECOMING BEST FRIENDS WITH YOUR HAMSTER, GUINEA PIG, OR RABBIT

BECOMING BEST FRIENDS WITH YOUR HAMSTER, GUINEA PIG. OR RABBIT

BY BILL GUTMAN

ILLUSTRATED BY ANNE CANEVARI GREEN

Pet Friends
The Millbrook Press
Brookfield, Connecticut

Published by The Millbrook Press, Inc.
2 Old New Milford Road
Brookfield, Connecticut 06804

Printed in the United States of America
5 4 3 2 1

Library of Congress Cataloging-in-Publication Data
Gutman, Bill.
Becoming best friends with your hamster, guinea pig,
or rabbit/by Bill Gutman:
illustrated by Anne Canevari Green.
p. cm.—(Pet friends)
Includes bibliographical references (p.   ) and index.
Summary: Explains in detail how to care for hamsters, guinea pigs,
and rabbits by providing an environment and diet
similar to the ones they would enjoy in nature.
ISBN 1-7613-0201-8 (lib. bdg.)
1. Hamsters as pets—Juvenile literature. 2. Guinea pigs as pets—Juvenile
literature. 3. Rabbits—Juvenile literature 4. Hamsters as pets—Behavior—Juvenile
literature. 5. Guinea pigs as pets—Behavior—Juvenile
literature. 6. Rabbits—Behavior—Juvenile literature.
[1. Hamsters. 2. Guinea pigs. 3. Rabbits. 4. Pets.]
I. Green, Anne Canevari, ill.   II. Title.
III. Series: Gutman, Bill. Pet friends.
SF459.H3G87 1997
636'.9332—dc20   96-31369. CIP AC

The author would like to thank

Dr. Alan Peterson, DVM,

*of Community Animal Hospital
in Poughkeepsie, New York,
for his careful reading of
the manuscript and his many
helpful comments and suggestions.*

UNDERSTANDING YOUR PETS

Animals have always played a major role in people's lives. In earlier days, animals did a great deal of work. Oxen pulled the plows that tilled the fields. Horses provided transportation. Dogs were used to guard people and herds of cattle or flocks of sheep. Wherever there were people, there were usually animals, too.

Today, animals are still a big part of many people's lives. Some still work. Others are kept in zoos or on game farms. And countless millions of animals are simply family pets.

There is much more to pet care than simple feeding and housing. Whether you have a dog, a cat, a bird, tropical fish, a hamster, a gerbil, a guinea pig, or even a horse or pony, you owe it to that animal to learn all you can about it. Obviously, animals can't tell you their feelings. You have to guess what they are thinking and feeling by the way they are acting—by their sounds, their movements, and by changes in their behavior.

This is very important if you want to have a happy, healthy pet that will live out its natural life span. The *Pet Friends* series will not only discuss basic animal care. It will also strive to show what your pet thinks and feels as it lives its life with you.

YOUR PET HAMSTER, GUINEA PIG, AND RABBIT

Hamsters, guinea pigs, and rabbits are three of the most popular pets in the world. The first two are members of the rodent family, while the rabbit is a related species. These small animals make ideal pets for younger children. A youngster can learn a great deal about animals by keeping and caring for any one of them.

Some people seem to have a natural dislike for these timid little animals. That's because their relatives in the wild are sometimes misunderstood. Rodents have always accounted for much disease and destruction in cities and around food supplies. Mice and rats (although they are also kept as pets) do not enjoy the best reputations in the animal world.

Rabbits, too, have been known to overpopulate certain areas and cause widespread destruction of crops. This can result in large losses of money for farmers. As a result, in many places people feel that the only good rabbit is a dead rabbit. And wholesale extermination of rabbits has taken place where the populations are out of control.

But, as in all of nature, animals are simply doing what comes naturally. That means following their instincts to survive. If a litter of baby mice is born in the basement of someone's home, the mice will eventually go upstairs to find food. Baby rabbits born in a den near a field of crops will soon turn to those crops for food.

Once again, it is sometimes difficult for animals and people to live side by side. When things get too crowded, it doesn't work. Yet under the right conditions, hamsters, guinea pigs, and

rabbits are wonderful little animals. It's fun to watch them transfer their instincts from the wild into your home.

But as with other pets, it's also your job to learn about them and understand their needs. In that way, you can provide an environment that allows them to do many of the things they would do if they were living in the wild.

If you do that, you will find that these pets will give you love and affection. You can watch them give birth and raise families. And you can provide safe and secure homes for animals that often live a dangerous and very short life in the wild.

HAMSTERS

The word hamster comes from the German *hamstern*, which means "to hoard." This describes one of the strongest instincts in all hamsters. They have a need to hoard food. They will stuff pouches in their cheeks with food, then hide the treasure in their cage until the time comes when they need it. Even when they have plenty of food every day as pets, they still love to hoard and hide it.

Hamsters have an unusual history. In 1930 a zoology professor found a female hamster and a litter of pups in a burrow in the

I'LL NEVER BE HUNGRY AGAIN...

13

Syrian desert. Syria is a Middle Eastern country bordering Israel. The climate is hot and dry. By the time the professor got the litter back to his laboratory, most of the hamsters had died or escaped.

But three survived, and four months later the first litter of golden hamsters was born in captivity. Then those babies were bred and before long there were thousands of domestic hamsters. Soon they were being used for research experiments.

Scientists liked the fact that the hamsters bred rapidly, were very hardy and healthy, and were easy to handle. By 1938, hamsters had been introduced to France and England, and finally to the United States. It is thought that nearly all golden hamsters in captivity today come from that first little family discovered in Syria.

The same characteristics that make hamsters good laboratory animals also make them excellent pets. Hamsters began to be kept as pets in the late 1940s. Today, there are millions of them in the United States alone.

THE JOY
OF HAMSTERS

Hamsters are thoroughly enjoyable little pets. They are inexpensive and easy to care for and give their owners countless hours of pleasure.

Though small, hamsters are larger than mice and have very pretty, appealing faces. They are also cuddly and easy to hold (although they will occasionally nip, especially if they smell food on your hands). They will stand up on their rear legs and amuse you with their ability to hold things with their front feet, which act almost like hands. They are clean, odorless animals and hardly ever utter a sound. No barking, meowing, screeching, chirping, or even squeaking.

You can also leave them alone for a few days and they will take perfect care of themselves. Hamsters don't have to drink much water, and since they love to hoard food, they will always have an extra supply on hand in their homes.

Even though hamsters don't have a long life span (approximately 1,000 days, or about 33 months), they usually remain healthy and hardy during that time. And they breed very rapidly.

A female hamster can have a litter of cubs just 16 days after mating with a male. So you can have an instant family and watch the mother raise the cubs.

WHAT ARE HAMSTERS LIKE?

Hamsters have a number of characteristics that they have brought from the wild. For instance, a hamster doesn't live as you and I do. It is a nocturnal animal, meaning that in the wild it sleeps by day and searches for food at night. Naturally, it will have to adapt somewhat to your way of living if you're going to be able to spend any time with it. If your hamster is sleeping and you want to play with it, wake it up slowly and gently. Keep it out of bright light until it is really awake.

If your hamster isn't happy about being awakened or is frightened, its ears will curl back. This is a warning sign. Keep talking gently to the animal until the ears stand up straight. Then it is all right to handle it.

VERY PRIVATE ANIMALS

In some ways, hamsters might be called solitary animals. Unlike dogs and other animals that like to gather in large groups, most hamsters love their privacy. They want privacy from other pets in the house, from humans, and sometimes from other hamsters.

The instinct for privacy is so strong that an adult female hamster has been known to attack and kill a male who was suddenly put into her cage at a time when she wasn't ready to breed. So always make sure that your hamster home has places where the hamster can hide from the world. Pet shops sell little houses and artificial caves where hamsters can find privacy.

If you have two or more hamsters in the same cage, make sure there are enough hiding places for each of them. If a hamster cannot get away from it all, feel safe and secure by itself, then it won't be happy. And if you have more than one hamster, separate them at the first signs of fighting.

In the wild, male hamsters live alone. Even when a male hamster is the father of a litter, he will not be involved in raising the cubs or in any family activities. Don't expect anything different in captivity.

THE HABIT OF HOARDING

A hamster will not simply eat and eat and eat. It seems to know that there may be times when food will not be abundant, and so it should save, or hoard, as much food as it can.

Nature has provided the hamster with a very clever way to do this. The hamster has a pouch in its cheeks that can hold large amounts of food. These unique pouches extend from the cheeks to the shoulder on both sides of the animal's mouth. Once the hamster is back in its home, it will deposit and hide the food in a safe place.

One thing to watch for: A hamster does not want the hidden food to be discovered or taken. If you should put your hand in the hamster's home and it's too near the food, the hamster may give you a nip.

OTHER CHARACTERISTICS

Like other rodents, hamsters do not have good eyesight. But they have super senses of smell and hearing. In fact, it is the sense of smell that guides many of the things hamsters do. It enables them to identify other hamsters, scent danger, become familiar with you, and search for food.

Hamsters are also sensitive to temperature. If you live in a warm climate where the temperature is often above 80 degrees Fahrenheit (27 degrees Celsius), your hamster may estivate—that is, fall into a very deep sleep, which might lead you to think

that your pet has died. Hamsters estivate to help them cope with the high heat in their native land. It's nature's way of helping furry animals survive in a hot, desert climate.

Hamsters are adventurous little animals. Having a natural curiosity, a hamster will always try to find a way out of its home. No matter how hard you try to prevent it, sooner or later almost every hamster seems to get out. Once out, hamsters can be very difficult to find. They may also be in danger from another family pet or, if they make it outside, from a variety of wild animals. So you must try to find your pet quickly.

Hamsters are very good at hiding. The best way to find them is to make your own trap. One method is to get a deep pail or wastebasket with smooth sides. Put some bedding and your pet's favorite food inside. Then make some kind of stairway or ramp so the hamster can get to the top of the pail. Put traces of the food on the steps.

If you set your trap at night before you go to bed, there's a good chance your hamster will be in the pail or basket in the morning. Remember, they are noctural animals and won't come out until the house is quiet and dark. Also remember to close the lids on toilets and cover aquariums and any other body of water. And if you have a cat, put it in a room where you're sure the hamster couldn't have gone.

WHAT'S THE BEST WAY TO HOUSE AND FEED MY HAMSTER?

Because a hamster is a small animal kept in a small enclosure, its care and feeding should not be difficult. But it's only easy if you know about the animal and its needs. As usual, you must try to give your hamster a lifestyle that comes as close as possible to its life in the wild.

Some hamster owners take pleasure in building their own enclosures for their pets. But for most first-time owners and those who just want a simple, well-designed home, it's best to buy one at a pet shop. Most commercial hamster homes are built with the animal in mind.

Fish aquariums have been used by some people, but they are not built to include some of the necessary accessories. The best type of cage is probably one that looks very much like a bird cage. It has a plastic tray on the bottom that slides out easily for cleaning and will not absorb urine, as a wood bottom enclosure will. Never use wood as flooring.

As with birds, the cage should be as large as possible. If it's too small, the hamster can become nippy. For a single animal, a cage that is 2 feet (60 centimeters) long, 18 inches (45 centimeters) deep, and 1 foot (30 centimeters) high is an ideal size.

BEDDING AND ACCESSORIES

The cage bottom should have an inch or two of a good, absorbent bedding. Use wood shavings or a commercial hamster litter. Hamsters love shredding newspaper, but the paper doesn't absorb as well as the other materials.

A feeding dish and water dispenser are also essential. The dish should not be too large and should hook onto the side of the cage so the animal can't dump it. Water should never be given in an open bowl. Hamsters don't drink that way in the wild.

In their desert home, hamsters drink drops of dew hanging from plants. They don't need a lot of water. So a water bottle, secured to the cage, with a glass tube for the water to drip from is the best method.

Another must is an exercise wheel on which the hamster can run. Hamsters absolutely need exercise. If they don't get it, they can actually become paralyzed. And don't be surprised if you hear your hamster running on the wheel at night. Remember, hamsters are noctural animals.

FOOD

Because hamsters love to gnaw, they enjoy eating hard foods slowly. They like hard grain such as corn, and love sunflower seeds and root vegetables such as carrots.

Hamsters also like some fresh soft foods, such as fruits and green vegetables. But these should not be given too often or allowed to be hoarded. Fresh foods can spoil or mildew and should be given only when the hamster can eat them quickly. Leftovers should be removed immediately.

Commercial hamster chows are available in pet supply stores and supermarkets. These are nutritionally balanced dry foods that won't spoil if the hamster hides some.

One feeding a day is usually enough, since the hamster can always go back to its hidden food supply. Many owners prefer to feed in the early evening when the animal is most active. This is when the hamster would be searching for food in the wild.

CLEANUP

Don't clean a hamster's cage too often. Daily cleanings will disturb your pet's hidden food and nest. It may lose its sense of privacy and begin to feel insecure. Once or twice a week is plenty, since hamsters usually urinate in just one spot and the rest of the cage will stay fairly clean.

SHOULD I BREED
MY HAMSTERS?

Breeding hamsters can be a joyful experience. The period from mating to birth is just sixteen days. That is the shortest for any mammal. A female hamster is in season and ready to breed every four days. Litters can be anywhere from two to fifteen cubs. The average is about eight. The cubs develop quickly and are mature hamsters in less than three months.

Babies are weaned (eating on their own) in about five weeks. Then just three to seven days after weaning, a female can breed again. Because the life cycle is so rapid, plan carefully if you decide to breed. Make sure that you can keep the cubs or find good homes for them. You don't want to continually breed your pets and suddenly find yourself with fifty hamsters and no place to keep them.

BREEDING BASICS

In the wild, hamsters mate in the dark, the cubs are born in the dark, and they spend their first few weeks in a dark nest at the end of a long burrow. The female's cage should have a nest box in a corner of the cage. Ask your pet-shop dealer about the best kind of box.

For mating, the female should be placed in the male's cage in the evening. Don't put the male in the female's cage. There is more of a chance that she will attack him violently if he comes into her space. Do not leave the male and female together overnight.

BRINGING UP BABIES

If you feel the breeding was successful, then just leave the female alone for at least nineteen days. If she has been bred, the babies will be born by then. The mother won't need help. Just keep the cage in a cool, dry place out of direct sunlight. Give the mother plenty of bedding, and enough food to both eat and hoard.

In some instances, a female hamster that is disturbed just before or within ten days of giving birth will attack and eat her young. Keep a close eye on her for the first few days so that you can remove the babies quickly if the mother shows signs of this behavior.

The babies should be able to reach the water tube as soon as their eyes are open. Make sure it isn't too high for them. Once the babies are eating on their own, they should be removed from the mother's cage. Males and females should be separated because they might try to breed almost immediately.

If you have other questions about breeding or raising the babies, ask your veterinarian or an experienced breeder.

KEEPING HAMSTERS HEALTHY

Hamsters are naturally hardy animals. With good care, a hamster should remain healthy throughout its lifetime. Cleanliness is the key. Keep food and water fresh and the cage clean. Don't let soft foods spoil or be hoarded.

Hamsters are vulnerable to some staph or strep bacterial infections. On rare occasions they might catch some of these illnesses from humans. A healthy, well-fed hamster is less likely to become sick, but don't take a chance. Try to avoid bringing your hamster to school, where crowded classrooms are full of sneezing kids.

Skin problems, parasites, and mites are all caused by poor hygiene. Constipation is a fairly common problem when only commercial hamster pellets are fed. If the animal isn't getting enough water, it may become constipated. Carrots, leafy vegetables, and fruits can help stop the problem.

Running eyes can mean there is food lodged in the cheek pouches by the shoulder. Soft foods get stuck more readily than hard foods. If this happens, you must flush out the pouches with warm water, using a syringe.

If your hamster develops a problem that puzzles you, check with a vet or an experienced keeper.

OLD AGE

Because hamsters have an average life span of about 1,000 days, they will not have a long old age. If your hamster is nearly three

years old and begins to show signs of illness, it may be time to take it to a vet and have it put to sleep humanely.

Since you have observed and cared for your hamster every day, you should be able to see the changes. If it stops eating, stops exercising, and doesn't seem to have its usual vitality, it may simply be getting old. It won't live much longer, and there is no sense letting your pet suffer. A responsible owner will know when it's time to say good-bye.

GUINEA PIGS

Guinea pigs come from the forests and grasslands of South America. They are also called "cavies," from their scientific name, *Cavia asperea*. These small rodents have been kept as pets for hundreds of years.

It is thought that the Spanish conquistadors brought the guinea pig to Europe in the sixteenth century. The conquistadors were returning from exploring countries in South America. The little animals adapted well to the European climate and became very popular as pets in a short time.

In the early to mid-eighteenth century, British sailors began to bring back guinea pigs from South American ports. When America was settled by the original colonists from Britain, guinea pigs came along for the ride.

Today, there are more than forty varieties of guinea pigs, created through selective breeding. One variety has short, straight hair; another has long, silky hair; and a third has coarse hair that grows in whorls. Guinea pigs are colored in various shades and patterns of black, brown, orange, and white.

Guinea pigs are larger than hamsters, closer to the size of a small rabbit. The average guinea pig is about 10 inches (25 centimeters) long and weighs about 3 pounds (1.4 kilograms).

GUINEA PIG APPEAL

Guinea pigs are cute and cuddly little animals. They are amusing and very curious about the world around them. They rarely bite or nip unless they are not handled properly. And they have a longer life span than the small rodents (hamsters and gerbils), often living well past six years of age.

Like many small animals, guinea pigs are naturally timid. But if you get a young one, preferably four to eight weeks of age (when it is weaned from mother's milk), you will have a gentle, affectionate pet. Young guinea pigs must be handled often and very gently so that they can gain confidence around humans.

Guinea pigs are easy to care for and can be lots of fun. They make an interesting variety of sounds, from squeaks to squeals to clucks. Females have small litters of four or five offspring, so if you breed your guinea pig you won't be swamped with babies and you will have an easier time finding homes for those you can't keep.

HOW DO I HOUSE AND FEED MY GUINEA PIG?

How you house your guinea pig depends somewhat on where you are going to keep it. If you have a single guinea pig and plan to keep it in the house, you can simply buy a cage from a pet shop. It probably will be rectangular in shape with metal bars and a plastic bottom that can be removed for easy cleaning. (A glass aquarium makes an excellent cage, although it is more difficult to clean.)

The cage should be placed in a location beyond the reach of other family pets. Guinea pigs cannot defend themselves against larger animals and are easily frightened by even the sight of jumping dogs and cats.

Get the largest cage or enclosure you can for your pet. As a rule, a single guinea pig needs an area at least 2 square feet (.19 square meters). In the wild, guinea pigs do not like to soil their living or sleeping areas. They will relieve themselves some distance away because they are clean animals. In a very small cage there will be no choice. This will make the animal unhappy and create an unhealthy environment.

A guinea pig also likes a sleeping area in which it feels safe and secure. It can be a homemade box, an earthenware pipe, or a clay flowerpot—just a place where your pet can sleep undisturbed or hide if something frightens it.

Sawdust is considered the best type of bedding because it absorbs urine well. You can use wood shavings, but they're not quite as absorbent. In the sleeping area, fresh hay (not straw) is an excellent choice because it is soft and warm. It is also a good food and gives the animal something extra to nibble on.

Drafts and dampness can cause health problems. Guinea pigs can withstand both warm and cold conditions as long as there are no drafts and their sleeping areas are fortified with warm, dry bedding.

Your guinea pig's home should also contain a heavy food dish or food chute and a water bottle with a tube, which will allow the guinea pig to drink a few drops at a time. In the wild, guinea pigs can get enough water from fresh vegetables and don't need to drink. But in captivity they must always have water available.

HUTCHES

Breeders and those who keep a large number of guinea pigs often make their own enclosures, or hutches. Hutches are usually made of wood and wire. The wood should be thick enough to be durable, at least half an inch. Weld wire is better than chicken wire because it keeps its shape, is stronger, and looks better. Make sure the wire is small enough to keep out other rodents, notably mice and rats that might get into your house or the building in which your guinea pigs are housed.

The hutch should be painted with a nontoxic paint. Use a number of coats on the base to seal it, so that any urine that goes through the bedding will not soak in. Some hobbyists use aluminum or plastic trays on the floor of the hutch to make cleaning easier.

It is also best to keep guinea pig hutches off the floor, on a table or shelf. That way, there is less chance of a draft, and you can view your pets more easily. If you have several hutches, you can stack them one on top of another.

Like other animals, guinea pigs need exercise. If you have one or two pets in the house, you can take them out of their cage and let them exercise in a closed room while you play with them. Or you can provide a cage large enough for exercise. But with many guinea pigs, it may be necessary to build an exercise area in which your guinea pigs can run.

This can be done by building an open pen indoors or a covered pen outdoors. Guinea pigs must always be protected from other animals—cats, dogs, other rodents, and outdoor animals such as skunks and raccoons.

The exercise or play area should contain items such as rocks, logs, maybe earthenware pipes. This will give the area a natural feel for the animals, as well as places to hide if they are frightened. That will make them feel more secure.

Remember, your guinea pig is going to spend a great deal of time in its home. Make it safe, comfortable, and roomy enough so that your pet is happy and healthy.

FEEDING

In technical terms, a guinea pig is an herbivore, meaning that it eats only vegetable matter, no meat. You can give your guinea pig many of your leftover vegetables—cooked, raw, and from cans. Just make sure to wash raw vegetables thoroughly to get rid of possible pesticides. And don't give your pets vegetables that have been pickled!

Commercial foods for guinea pigs are also available, usually in the form of pellets, that contain a balance of vitamins and minerals. Some experts feel that you shouldn't feed such pellets exclusively. Variety is better for your pet, both physically and mentally. Let your guinea pig have fun with its food.

Foods are divided into two categories—dry and soft. Dry foods include the pellets, oats, bran, and wheat products such as stale bread, toast, and crackers. Guinea pigs also enjoy shelled nuts. Cheese and scrambled eggs are also in the dry category and can be made into a mash for your pet.

Soft foods include fruits and vegetables that have a high percentage of liquid. Apples, oranges, strawberries, and berries are examples of healthy fruits. Celery, carrots, potatoes, broccoli, lettuce, and grasses (especially alfalfa) are also good for guinea pigs.

You should feed with a set routine, such as the morning and late afternoon. Then your pet will squeal with delight when it sees its food coming. Dry foods, such as pellets, should be available at all times.

One other note: Along with monkeys, apes, and people, the guinea pig is the only known mammal that cannot manufacture vitamin C in its body. So make sure you provide food that is specifically labeled as guinea pig food. Gerbil or rabbit food will not contain adequate vitamin C. Supplements are also available. In addition, you can buy mineral blocks that contain salts and other essentials. Put one of these blocks in each cage—your guinea pig will appreciate it.

Of course, fresh water should always be available. Clean the water bottle daily and be sure to rinse it thoroughly. Follow these few simple feeding rules, and your guinea pig should remain well fed, happy, and healthy.

THE FUN OF
BREEDING

There is a very interesting difference between breeding guinea pigs and hamsters. The period from mating to birth for guinea pigs is much longer, approximately 61 to 64 days. The babies are born with fur already covering their bodies. Their eyes are open, and they can run around and eat a little guinea pig food on their own within just hours of being born.

The female (called a sow) can mate every 16 days or so. Thus a male (called a boar) can be left with her for a number of weeks and mate several times. If you see the female gaining weight, you can assume she is carrying babies. It's a good idea to give the mother more food than usual prior to breeding to ensure that she will have enough vitamins and minerals to see her through.

Some breeders leave a number of guinea pigs together to breed as a colony, and sometimes both sow and boar will take care of the babies. But you can never be sure that there won't be fighting. If you are breeding two pets for the first time, it's best to remove the female to her own enclosure as soon as you suspect that she is pregnant.

Some people will breed the sow again as soon as her litter is born. This is not a good idea, since the mother is still nursing and needs several weeks to fully regain her strength and vitality.

One word of warning: A guinea pig sow must be bred before the age of six months. If she is bred for the first time after that age, her pelvic area may not expand properly to allow natural birth.

DEALING WITH THE BABIES

Because guinea pig babies are not totally helpless at birth, they are easier to deal with than hamster babies. The mother will still give them plenty of attention. She will lick them clean, let them dry, then keep them warm with her body. These are all instinctive behaviors.

The sow has just two milk glands. So if there are more than two babies, they must take turns suckling. You have to watch to make sure there isn't a weaker baby who isn't getting enough milk. If you have to help feed a weak baby, use diluted canned evaporated milk. You can feed the baby from a small spoon, or soak some bread in boiling water, drain the water, and add some milk. Let the mixture cool before feeding.

Within just four to five weeks, the babies are weaned and can live and eat on their own. They can be removed from the mother's enclosure and put in one of their own. If you aren't going to keep them, this is the time to send them to their new homes.

WHAT'S WRONG WITH MY GUINEA PIG?

As with all small mammals, the most common cause of illness in guinea pigs is a lack of cleanliness in their surroundings. Spoiled food, damp and soiled bedding, and overcrowding in a hutch can cause your pets to become ill. In fact, the more pets you keep, the more important cleanliness becomes.

In the case of guinea pigs, disease can be spread by direct contact. An illness can be carried on your hands from a sick animal to a healthy one if you don't wash your hands well. This is very important when you have many pets.

It's also a good idea to wash a new animal coming into your home if you've already got guinea pigs there. It might have picked up disease organisms in the pet shop. You might also wash an animal after you take it to a show or even a friend's house if the friend has guinea pigs. It's certainly better to be safe than sorry.

A hutch floor that is not sealed can also cause disease. Bacteria can form if urine soaks into the floor of the hutch or food matter gets into cracks. If you don't clean the hutch regularly, flies and other insects will gather and can cause illness in

your guinea pig. In the wild, the animal can abandon a soiled or dirty home. In captivity, it can't.

Do not leave soft food and fresh vegetables in the hutch for more than a few hours. If it isn't eaten, take it out. Decaying food is another breeding ground for illness-causing bacteria.

Watch for symptoms of illness. If your pet has a runny nose or watery eyes, seems to have difficulty breathing, has any signs of blood in the urine or feces, or develops bald patches on the skin, call your vet immediately. Also, if you have more than one guinea pig, remove the sick animal and place it in a room and cage by itself. Then call the vet.

As a rule, guinea pigs do not catch diseases from humans. So if you're coughing or sneezing you can still cuddle with your guinea pig.

If your guinea pig is more than six years old, watch it even more carefully. If it seems to be slowing down, has trouble moving around, doesn't want to play, or isn't eating well, it might be time to say good-bye. Your veterinarian, who wants only the best for your pet and you, will know if it's time to put your old friend to sleep.

RABBITS

There was a time when rabbits were considered rodents. Rabbits have two pairs of big gnawing teeth in the front of the jaw, like rodents. But they also have a second pair of upper incisors. These are small teeth almost hidden by the large gnawing teeth in front. Rodents do not have these smaller teeth. For this reason and others, rabbits are now placed in a separate category from rodents.

THE GOOD NEWS IS THAT YOU'RE NOT A RODENT. THE BAD NEWS IS THAT WITH ALL THESE TEETH, YOU NEED BRACES.

There are twenty-five species of rabbits. Domestic rabbits have been bred for years, and at least forty breeds are recognized in America. Over the years, rabbits have been used as food, and they still are to a large extent. It wasn't until the early 1900s that tame rabbits were first brought to America.

The most common wild rabbit in North America is the eastern cottontail, which is about 16 inches (40 centimeters) long and weighs between 2 and 4 pounds (0.9 and 1.8 kilograms). A female bears several litters every year, each consisting of four to six babies.

The cottontail is a natural prey for many other animals, such as the fox and coyote. And they are targets for more human hunters in the United States than all big game combined. But the cottontail is a resourceful animal that has survived to hold its own against its enemies.

WHAT MAKES RABBITS GOOD PETS?

Nearly everyone living in a rural area undoubtedly has seen wild rabbits sitting in the yard sunning themselves or munching on vegetation. They may let you approach them, but when you get too close, they run off.

Wild rabbits are almost impossible to tame as pets. But rabbits bred in captivity make excellent pets for both children and adults.

Since rabbits are larger than hamsters and guinea pigs, they're easier to play with. In fact, they enjoy being picked up and petted. They also have a longer life span than the smaller animals, usually eight to ten years, so they will be with you for a longer time.

Rabbits are very clean animals, always grooming themselves. They are quiet, can be kept indoors or outside, have few veterinary needs, rarely bite, and can be surprisingly affectionate.

It is estimated that more than 12 million rabbits are raised in the United States each year. And more than 50,000 men, women, and children belong to the American Rabbit Breeders Association. Many more raise rabbits without belonging to the Association.

Raising rabbits is a popular hobby. And with so many people enjoying the hobby and keeping rabbits as pets, the rabbit must be doing something right.

WHAT'S FIRST?

The first thing you have to do is decide what kind of rabbit you want. Wild cottontails are small animals, but some of the domestic breeds are quite large. You can buy a dwarf rabbit no larger than a guinea pig, or you can get a giant breed that weighs up to 20 pounds (9 kilograms), larger than many breeds of toy dogs.

So before getting a pet rabbit, ask questions and try to observe the different breeds in person. Think about the space where the rabbit will be kept, the time you'll be spending with it, and the money you will have available for food and supplies. It costs more to maintain a 15- or 20-pound (7- or 9-kilogram) rabbit than one that weighs just a few pounds.

There are a lot of rabbits to choose from, so don't buy one on a whim. Think it through, learn about the breeds, and seek as much expert advice as you can.

HOUSING

Domestic rabbits are not like their wild cousins. They are not used to running and hopping long distances every day, so the pet rabbit doesn't need a lot of room in its hutch.

Some breeders and keepers prefer an all-wire hutch. They worry that if the hutch is made of wood, their rabbits may gnaw on it and possibly be harmed by splinters or by ingesting the wood itself. But many rabbits will leave the wood alone or gnaw only a little. A little gnawing can serve to sharpen the teeth, which can be a good thing. If your rabbit is gnawing all the time, to the point where you feel it may be harmful, then you can switch to an all-wire hutch.

A hutch can be bought or built. When building a hutch, here are some other things to consider:

- A rabbit needs clean quarters.

- It needs light and ventilation, but it cannot be in winds or drafts.

- A rabbit can withstand the cold, but suffers in hot, humid weather.

- A rabbit cannot tolerate dampness or a wet floor. Dampness can make it sick.

- A rabbit should be protected from dogs, cats, and any wild animals in the area.

WANNA COME OUT AND PLAY ?

With an all-wire hutch, droppings and urine pass through to a box or tray that can be easily cleaned. Only an occasional wire brushing and disinfecting are necessary to keep the hutch clean. Rabbits are very clean animals, always grooming and washing themselves. Only when they are not in an all-wire hutch do they appear dirty.

Outdoor hutches need protection from the wind and rain. If a rabbit is outdoors or in a cold building, its fur will become thicker to protect it. There should also be a fence at least 4 feet (1.2 meters) high around the hutch to prevent other animals from trying to get at your rabbit. In cold weather, you can put some bedding into the hutch, such as straw or fresh shavings. You can also put a wooden box in the hutch for short periods, but remove it if it becomes damp.

LETTING A RABBIT LOOSE

If you keep your rabbit in the house and want to let it out of the hutch to play with it, you must be very careful. Always stay with your rabbit and watch it closely. Rabbits will gnaw on furniture and other pieces of wood. They may also gnaw on electrical cords, which can be a danger to them and you.

Don't bring a rabbit in from the cold, play with it in a warm room, then put it out again. The sudden change in temperature can make it susceptible to a cold or pneumonia.

If you want to let the rabbit loose outside, make sure your pet will allow you to handle it. Otherwise, you might have a great

deal of trouble catching it to bring it back inside. Also be sure the area is fenced and is free of poisonous plants. (Young rabbits, under six months of age, should not even eat green grass.)

A domestically raised rabbit does not have the built-in defense mechanisms of its wild cousins. It can get in big trouble fast if left alone.

HOW DO I FEED MY RABBIT?

Remember Bugs Bunny? That famous cartoon character would do anything for a carrot. Other rabbits in comics and cartoons were always munching carrots, as well. But if you feed your rabbit nothing but carrots, it will not get the vitamins and minerals it needs to keep healthy.

Much has been learned about animal nutrition. With a little care and knowledge, it shouldn't be hard to feed your rabbit and keep it healthy for its entire lifetime.

Rabbit pellets, available in grocery and pet stores, can be the staple of the diet and fed every day. But while these pellets claim to give the rabbit a complete and balanced diet, supplemental roughage in the form of alfalfa, timothy hay, and fibrous vegetables and fruits are necessary for the animal's health.

Begin to introduce these supplements when the rabbit is about six months old. Younger bunnies can have some timothy hay as a daily treat, but the other foods (except for the pellets) contain too much moisture for baby intestinal tracts to handle. Wash all fruits and vegetables thoroughly with plain water before serving, to remove any pesticides that might have been sprayed on them.

Introduce new foods slowly and in small amounts. Don't suddenly give a whole apple or carrot to a rabbit that has never had it before. Too much of a new food can disrupt the normal bacterial flora and cause sudden death due to "toxic shock."

As with other animals, make sure that fresh drinking water is available at all times.

HARDY ANIMALS

Rabbits are naturally hardy animals if you keep them supplied with nutritious food, fresh water, and clean conditions. But you should still watch for a few things.

There are two ailments that rabbits can pass on to humans. One is a parasite called ringworm. If you observe that your rabbit's fur is falling out, leaving circular patches, don't handle the rabbit until you get medication from your veterinarian. Ringworm is not difficult to cure.

Another ailment is scabies, or mange. This is caused by small insects called mites. The rabbit will scratch itself around the infected area until the fur is worn away. You will soon see a yellowish, crusty scab around the area. Once again, this is easy to treat with medication and advice from your vet.

Another way to avoid problems is to house just one rabbit per hutch. You may feel sorry for your pet and want to give it a buddy. However, two male rabbits will often fight, and while two females won't fight as often, they would still need to be watched. And, of course, if you keep a male and female together you may end up with a lot of baby rabbits you don't want.

The most common ailment of domestic rabbits is coccidiosis. This is an infection that can kill young rabbits or retard their growth. The symptoms are diarrhea, a bloated belly, and a lack of gloss and a general roughness of the fur. A medication you can get from your veterinarian, sulfaquinoxaline sodium, controls this infection.

One dangerous disease that rabbits can get is pasteurellosis, or "snuffles." It is a bacterial infection usually caused by stress. Animals shipped together in crowded conditions often contract this illness. It causes a high fever, breathing difficulty, and eventually pneumonia. If you suspect this, call your vet immediately. Snuffles is treated with antibiotics, which the vet must prescribe.

Also keep an eye on your rabbit's feet. Some rabbits like to stomp on the cage floor. A wire floor can cause sore or ulcerated

back feet, which must be treated by a vet. You might have to put a wooden stomping board on the floor of the hutch to protect your pet's feet.

HOW ABOUT BABIES?

Rabbits may be rewarding to breed, but breeding is not necessarily for everyone. Keeping one rabbit is easy. Two is a little more work, but not much. Then suddenly you have a litter of babies. After two or three months with their mother, each young rabbit will need its own hutch. Your rabbit world has now expanded, and so has the work and the expense.

Plan carefully. If you want to breed, decide what kind of rabbits you hope to get. If you have one rabbit, obviously you must get another of the opposite sex and probably the same breed.

The female, or doe, needs a hutch that has as many square feet of floor as she weighs. So if the doe weighs 5 pounds (2.3 kilograms), the area of the hutch must be 5 square feet (.46 square meters). You will also need a nest box after the mating has taken place. You can buy a wire box with cardboard liners, or make a wooden one. Never use a plain cardboard box because the doe may eat it. You will also need a second hutch to house the male, or buck, after the babies are born.

Rabbits are territorial animals, and does can be more territorial than bucks. Always bring the doe to the buck's cage for mating. If you bring the buck to the doe, the doe may be more interested in defending her territory than in mating.

It takes an average of 31 days between mating and birth. Baby rabbits begin growing fur in two days and are fully furred in about two weeks. Their eyes open in about 10 days. You can begin handling the babies at about three weeks. By about eight weeks the babies will be weaned and eating pellets. Remove only half the litter from the doe at one time, and then a few days later remove the other half. That way, the doe's body adjusts to reduced milk production.

Once again, you will have the responsibility of finding homes for your babies. If you keep them, each will need its own hutch. If not, you might be able to sell them to a local pet shop or to a professional breeder. If this is not possible, find them good homes. Never just let them go. They won't join their wild cottontail cousins and enjoy romping in the woods. It doesn't work that way. Once a rabbit is a pet, it's always a pet.

Small animals, such as hamsters, guinea pigs, and rabbits, are 100 percent dependent on you for everything! They cannot survive on their own. You must house them, feed them, keep them clean, and interact with them. These little animals may not live as long as other pets, but they still deserve a good, happy life. It is always the responsibility of you, the pet owner, to learn something about these animals before you buy them, so that you are ready to satisfy their natural needs.

FIND OUT MORE

Barkhausen, Annette, and Franz Geiser. *Rabbits and Hares.* Milwaukee: Gareth Stevens, 1994.

Jameson, Pam, and Tina Hearne. *Responsible Pet Care Series.* Vero Beach, FL: Rourke Publications, 1989.

King-Smith, Dick. *I Love Guinea Pigs.* Cambridge, MA: Candlewick Press, 1995.

McPherson, Mark. *Choosing Your Pet.* Mahwah, NJ: Troll Associates, 1985.

Piers, Helen. *Taking Care of Your Hamster.* Hauppauge, NY: Barron, 1992.

INDEX